T0198817

The Blessing

I'm Going to Heaven!

Written & illustrated by:

Tina M. Lowe

To order additional copies of this book, contact:
Xlibris
844-714-8691
www.Xlibris.com
Orders@Xlibris.com

ISBN: Softcover   978-1-6641-5561-9
         EBook   978-1-6641-5560-2

Print information available on the last page

Rev. date: 01/30/2021

The Blessing, I'm Going to Heaven!

Written & Illustrated by: Tina M. Lowe

Introduction

This is the First book that I am publishing out of my Collection of Poetry I have written throughout the years. It is the Seventh book out of seven. Since 1999, I have been writing Poetry. It is my Escape and way of expressing how I feel at that time and moment. Writing is my turn to and coping mechanism to deal with events or situations that is going on in my Life. The Collection altogether is called "The Inner Thoughts." The year 2020 was a very challenging year for me. It tested the deepest part of my Heart, Mind, Soul and Faith in the things I believed in the most. I overcame all of them. I came out of the Storm Stronger and more Will-Powered to conquer anything that comes in the path of my Journey to find Inner Peace and Myself!

I Dedicate this Book to:

My "Angel up above", My Beautiful Mommy
up in Heaven, May she be looking down on me
every day and was taken home way too soon!
"My Mommy B.K.A Ruth Ann Kraushaar!"
~12.10.1964-7.14.2019~

Table of Contents

Chapter 1: <u>No Love Lost!</u>

~Enough is enough~ 2

Shielded w/Distance 3

"Love is a Battlefield!" 4

~Healing Heart~ 5

A Friendship Conquers 6

Packed Away! 8

~In sync as One~ 10

Letting Go! 12

Numb! 13

Lost – n – Confused with so many Emotions 14

The Sound of my Heart being Broken! 16

Should have. 18

~Lost Love~ 19

No Love Lost! 20

Chapter 2: _Family: Through Thick – n – Thin_

Birthday Wishes up to Heaven! 22

Quarantine 25

~Guidance~ 26

Trials ~N~ Tribulations of my Journey 27

Life Vs Reality...28

Chapter 3: _Myself: The Battle from WITHIN_

Windows 30

My Inner Self...31

Value of my Worth! 33

~ Lost ~ 34

To Conquer Self –Love 35

~Twisted Madness~ 37

~Empty Vessel~ 38

Shattered! 40

Ecstatic with a Damaged Soul! 41

~Enough is enough~

When it comes to Love, don't let it show again. Learn to let go of the feelings that should no longer be there! Stop shedding tears for someone that doesn't shed them for you or even take your feelings into consideration. Teach yourself how to walk away when you're not wanted by them, the way you want them.

Today is the day, where I free my Heart of the Pain I put it through not them! We do it to ourselves because we know where we stand with them. It's time to dry those eyes, let go of the painful feelings and emotions that we feel to be strong enough to Walk Away!!

Shielded w/ Distance

You're a good woman with a Heart of Gold and know one day maybe soon, someone will cherish your Heart like you cherish theirs. They'll reciprocate the love you have for them and make you feel like you NEVER were Loved before! It's going to feel great and your Heart and Soul will be happy! So today, take that one step closer to not feel deeply for an individual who doesn't want you.

Show them that you no longer crave for them, yearn for their Love or cry because of heartache. You're strong and too good of a person to let Love break you like this. Don't ever give your Heart to an individual anymore unless you know deep down that they are not going to crush it!!

"Love is a Battlefield!"

People say "Love is a Battlefield!" They sure are right. We fight to be loved the right way; we want to feel it and not have to second guess it! You may get hurt, knocked down but in the end, don't let it kill your Soul! I am going to win this battle and move on in life, with my Integrity attached. The ball is in my Court now for I have the leverage!

So, just wish them the best and leave on a good note to where they know I will always have a special place in my Heart for them. As far as being in Love and having strong feelings for them, it should No Longer be allowed!

~Healing Heart~

    You know that letting go of all the Love and Feelings that once was there will hurt at first but I shall not shed any tears. After time passes, your Heart will start to heal from all the Pain and Anguish it had endured. I will fight this battle of Love and conquer it with Healing from letting go of them along with all the feelings that you once had for them!!

A Friendship Conquers

What do you do when your Heart, Mind and Soul is put to the test?

What do you do when there are only two questions to answer but you're the only one who can solve either question?

What matters most at the end of your day?

Is it the friendship that you first started out with? The laughing, joking around, enjoying each other's company and everything wasn't so serious. Or is it the part where you fell in Love with someone you felt you had a bond with?

(Continued on Pg.7)

They're one of the few people that can turn your frown upside right and will make you feel complete just by being in their presence, knowing that they may not feel the same way about you.

I ultimately would choose Friendship because Relationships don't always last but friendships can last for an eternity! To just have someone by your side, to talk to, to be able to BS with and just have a good time with. It's the Simple things in life that matter most to me! I've always been bad at Love. So, now a friendship is what I strive for.

You pack up what's left in your Heart and Mind of what was, keep on caring for them but the deep Love, feelings and all the memories will be stored away and Never to be opened again!

Packed Away!

I am going to pack my feelings away in suitcase, walk it to the bridge, toss it over and watch it just float away! As I stand there numb, it is getting further away to where I can barely see the suitcase anymore. I am going to strip the Love right out of my Heart and shred it into millions of pieces, until there is no way of ever putting it back together again. These memories are just thoughts of what was. I am slowly deleting the moments we had together.

I am staring a blank stare into the midair with no tears streaming down my cheeks; no pain in my Heart, no yearning for the attention anymore, just a cold bitter stare that is numb to her and a thing called "Love"!

(Continued on Pg.9)

With no point of ever to return or come back in my mind, it is easing into a lonely place but a Sanitarium. They say it is better to love then to not love at all! I experienced it first hand and learned love is no for me.

So, at the end of the end of the day when my Heart may be lonely my mind is my sanitarium where it is at peace without love and I am ok with that. I fell in love with two people in my life I felt and experienced it and I know love is not the main thing in life. When the day comes to an end, my Integrity and strong will is what truly matters!

~In sync as One~

What is it to love someone but don't really have that genuine love for them anymore?

Why is it when you can look at somebody, be able to tell that you don't mean as much to them as they mean to you and can feel it deep in your gut too?

Why do these feelings fade further away into a Cold Dark place?

Why do I have these feelings not of Anguish or Despair but of revenge and rivalry?

(Continued on Pg.11)

My Heart, Mind and Soul are all in sync. We know what we deserve, where we belong, who truly wants us and want the feeling of belongingness! I am following to where it makes sense not to where I used to be wanted anymore!

In the end when your Heart, Mind and Soul works as one, that's when you find out the truth of the path you took. It either shows you that it was the right one or shows you it's not where you belong!

Letting Go!

They say when you love someone so deep that all that matters is their happiness, Let them go! Even if it isn't with you that make them happy, you let go of them, all feelings and everything you had with them. You free them to be happy in life. When you let them go, you're happy knowing they're living their life happier and you feel content with the decision of letting them go!

I think that is all the corrections needed. When I receive the final copy to sign off on, will go over it again.

Numb!

My Heart is Cold, Mind is Numb and Soul is Lost. I feel freaking numb to the world! My emotions are out of Control! I am looking out with only my eyes. They're screaming screw the World, screw being nice and screw ever trusting anyone again like I did before, screw a relationship and screw Love, Not worth a damn to me anymore!

Especial fuck anyone who thinks it's cool to treat people wrong and they deserve a Silver Platter. I am screaming that's so loud from deep down in my Soul, with all my Heart and every bit of my Mind that it fucking hurts internally!

Lost – n – Confused with so many Emotions

As my sad Heart is aching, it is screaming out with so much Pain N Sorrow!

As my Heart is breaking, the tears are streaming down my cheeks w/so much Force!

As my Soul feels all alone, my whole body Trembles N Shakes!

As my Mind is filled with worry N Concern, I don't know which way to turn!

From the day I met you, I can still picture you walking up my steps into my front door. I saw something in you that were Good N Genuine. That is rare to find. You had a good personality.

(Continued on Pg.15)

Your face so filled with life N a Smile that could brighten up the room as you walked in! We would be able to just sit back, laugh N enjoy each other's company!

For me, I so Miss the person that I met that day N grew a bond with! You're not the same no more for I don't know what to do anymore! I wish I was an Angel that can just scoop you up, take you in my arms N show you what a wonderful person you are! Oh, that day was a wonderful day, it's like we just clicked!'

Now I sit here N wonder if I will ever see the old you again? I wonder if the old you is gone with no point of ever returning? I can be there for you but it'll have to be just from a distance! You have a Ring that I bought you to remind you of my existence. For every day that I got to spend with you, was a day that we never wasted! We laughed so hard together, what such wonderful unforgettable times we shared!

The Sound of my Heart being Broken!

When I gave you my Heart N put it in your hands to cherish, it was so full of Life, Love N beating w/Joy! You took it N eventually little by little started to squeeze it. As time passed, you squeezed it a bit harder. My Heart opened like a wound N the insides just started coming out. My Heart started aching N filled w/so much confusion! Then more time passed, you squeezed harder N it busted open. My blood is just gushing right out. All the insides of my Heart crying out in pain! When it got to that point N there was nothing left to come out of it! What was I left with? I was left w/a Hollow shaped form of a Heart that once was full of Life N Love!

It is now dead N empty to the Core!! It is becoming numb to the feelings I once had for you, ending up with nothing left in there! My Heart started to dry up N eventually started to harden. It is now filled w/anguish N is more vulnerable to beat slower! Over time it completely dried out, turned black, started to get cold N dying slowly.

(Continued on Pg.17)

My Heart was getting used to the pain N no longer crying out w/ such Sadness! As my Heart eventually died w/no point of return. It got cold, so cold that when you touched it, you got Frostbite! Once my Heart froze, there is no warming or filling it back up w/all that once was inside my Heart before you squeezed everything out of it w/your Disregard for my feelings N made me feel irrelevant to you!

You striped the Life, the Love N Joy right out of my Heart. My Mind N Soul became one N numb to forget all of the pain that you put my Heart through! So now all you're left w/is this Numb Bitter Cold-Hearted Bitch of a woman that can give two fucks about a damn thing in life but yourself! You made a Loyal, Good Hearted woman that once Loved N Cared very deeply for you into a Woman Scorned that doesn't no longer care if you're Alive or Dead! How does it make your Soul feel as a Man to turn a Woman's Heart that once was pure N full of Love into a Heart that is Dark N full of Hatred?

Should have . . .

When I wanted to walk away from you years ago, you should of just Let Me Go and Live My Life but you didn't. You didn't want me to walk away then but Now it's a Whole Different Tune! You don't want me in your life like that now!

If you were so fucked up on what you wanted all these Years, you then should have been a Grown Ass Man, been straight up with me and Told Me! I would have just straight fucking walked away from you and left out of your life to Never Look Back! I could have actually been Happy Right Now with someone who does want Me but No you Played me like a fucking Game and thought it was Funny. This Shit isn't No Joke and it's far from Fucking Funny!!

~Lost Love~

You should have straight up just let go of me, so I can move on w/ my fucking life. I wouldn't be like this right now. I wouldn't be filled w/so much Anger and Hatred!! No, you played my Heart like a fiddle, used my Body like it was your playground, Turned my Soul inside out and it became a Maze. I lost myself along the way trying to love someone not worthy of My Love.

My Mind, that Bitch is Destroyed! Best believe Sadness and Disregard destroyed my Mind but the sadness has now gone and left. It is the Anger, Anguish, Madness and just the whole thought of you couldn't Respect Me when I wanted to Walk Away for my Own Happiness!! Instead of you letting me walk away to be happy in My Life, you asked me to Stay! I was very Stupid for sticking around for your Dumbass!

No Love Lost!

I will Never be stupid again! Best believe that you made me more Strong-Willed to not be stupid ever again for anyone. I will have a Good Life, Family that loves me and maybe soon I will have someone who actually wholeheartedly Loves me for Me! They won't bullshit me; won't play with my Heart or Mind like it's their toy. They'll be Straight Up with me and be Honest.

So, I'm leaving it at this when my Heart and Mind told me to walk away from you, you should have Respected Me enough and just Let Me Go!

5

Birthday Wishes up to Heaven!

Your day grows near that you were Blessed with Life and I am very distraught! I am very Sad that I can't see your Beautiful Face smiling at me on your day! I miss being able to just call you up on your day to wish you a Happy Birthday and tell you how much I Love You Mommy! Oh, how I miss your warm embrace every time you hugged me, for they were truly valued very much so! I remember the sound of your laughter just like it was yesterday, that I heard you laughing!

The Love you gave me throughout my Life until the day you went Home was unconditional. I cherish your Love every day!

(Continued on Pg. 23)

The things in Life that you taught me and how to achieve my goals throughout my Life, Never goes unnoticed! Also the way you showed me how to be Strong-Willed, keep my Will Power and to stay positive in Life, are very much appreciated! All the things you have done for me, taught me and showed me throughout your Lifetime here with me, I apply to my everyday life!

So, this is a Big Shout Out to my Mommy up in Heaven with so much Love on her day! I was your Miracle Baby and you will Always be my Best Friend as well as my Beautiful Mother that I was Blessed with! I am Grateful every day for you being a huge part in my Life for I know you're looking down on me. Happy Birthday to my "Angel Up Above"! I Love and miss you dearly!!

Family: Through Thick N Thin Pg.23

(This Poem is Dedicated to my Beautiful Mother and Best Friend who was taken too soon from me!)

Live, Laugh, Love

6

Quarantine

I thought life was harder before all this happened! Every day I wake up to see the changes Socially, Environmentally and just the differences that have been made in my life. There may not have been a whole lot of changes but they were Drastic! Not a lot of traffic on the roads and not too many people walking on the streets. There is a curfew set for people to be inside by a certain time. It's like being in a Horror Film that became a reality. It's Terrifying and makes me shiver down to my Bones! You know how to survive but the thought of it all Torments my Soul! All I do is Pray to the Lord up above for a fresh new start after all this is over!

~Guidance~

I am on a Journey to find Myself and my Soul. You showed me I had a purpose on this Earth when I was in a Dark, Cold like tunnel trying to find my way back Home. You showed me the light to follow! I trusted you, so I followed and it led me back to my Body. For that I am the utmost appreciative of you giving me Life! You guide me through this Storm I am going through and come out knowing I Found myself, my soul and Inner Peace once again. Thank you for being there for me Spiritually, helping me save myself from drowning in this World and Not giving up on myself when times get tough!

Trials ~N~ Tribulations of my Journey

Instead of looking at a picture as a whole, pick an object out of the image and focus on it. As you're focusing on the object you analyze it as an individual item and begin to understand that all of the smaller things we do in our lives add up to one's Reflection of Thyself as a whole. As well as understand everything that happens to us in Life, is one of many we may encounter. In the End they all sum up my Trials ~N~ Tribulations of my Journey through this thing called "Life"!

Life Vs Reality

What is this thing that I call my life? It is the Cold - N -Numbness that I walk around feeling like you're worthless and just knowing that you can't fake it until you make it. I stay optimistic to look forward to a brighter Future! Reality sets in and shows me very well that I am a very Lost Soul. I am stuck in a maze trying to find my way back home, have a Heart filled with Contentment once and for all!

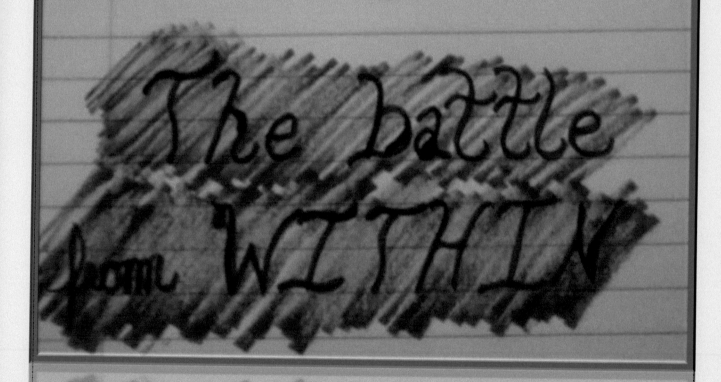

7

Windows

My eyes are not just Blue and used for sight to see but they are like my windows to the outside World. I see life outside of Myself. I see things the way I know the way they should be as well as things I need and want in life. There are the things that may make me sad, angry, lonely and make me not feel like myself. What can I change with using my eyesight as my windows? I can change things that I know will make a difference!

January 28, 2020

My Inner Self

As the Thunder rolls inside my Head, my Heart is breaking.

As the rain is pouring down on my Head, my Tears are rolling down my Cheeks.

As the Wind is blowing me around, I am Mentally Unstable.

When the Lightning strikes, I am facing Insanity and Madness from within my Soul!

As the Hail is coming down, I am filled with so much Anger.

When the Fog comes rolling in, I can't see anything, Confusion and Uncertainty starts to set in!

(Continued on Pg. 32)

The Clouds are heavy and Grey, I am feeling so Lonely.

As the Snowflakes fall all around me, my Heart is Frozen shut!

When the Sun eventually comes out shining brightly, my Heart is filled with Contentment and Joy.

When the sky is Clear, I can see things with Certainty and I am filled with Reassurance!

While I am expressing my Feelings Externally they all depend on the Weather Internally. If I put all the weather together they can become one of three different scenarios. They can be equal to a Storm before the Calm brewing inside of my Mind with Catastrophe attached destroying my Soul or I can be in the Eye of the Storm where it's neutral but I know it's not over yet. I can also beat the Storm by becoming stronger and reach the Calm after the storm when it's over. I will be filled with Calmness like the Ocean with my Heart Content being at Peace within Itself!

May 18. 2020

Value of my Worth!

Listen to the facts, My Worth doesn't decrease in value by the lack of someone else's value of my worth. My value according to someone else doesn't matter at the end of the day. I know my Worth and its value is of every damn dime. Not one Soul on this Earth is going to make me feel less than that! If anyone can't see the Value of my Worth and doesn't accept me for me, it is Their Loss not Mine!

~ Lost ~

I don't know where to turn, when I have people in my Life Physically but not Mentally!

I don't know who to talk to, when there are people around me but can care less!

How do I shut my Mind off without starting to not Care for the people that mattered the most to me?

How can I make my Heart at Peace without giving up all the feelings that I once felt?

So, to find my way back Home, is to turn off my Mind and lose all the feelings that once was and hope for the best!

To Conquer Self – Love

To Conquer Self – Love we have to remind ourselves at times of the traits we possess. Sometimes we must also have little pep talks within ourselves to reassure us that as long as we love ourselves, we will conquer self-love!

So, remember to always Smile! You are and will always be Beautiful inside and out. You have a great personality and a Heart of Gold. You're a great person to be around, if treated right! Always know when to walk away from the things that is killing your Heart, Mind, Soul and Spirit deep down inside!

(Continued on Pg. 36)

At the end of each day, always know your Worth and never let anyone make you feel less of your Value! Remember to Love thyself first because if you don't love yourself truly, you can't love someone else. Last but not least Care for your Heart, Mind and Soul because they are what makes you Genuinely who you are! No one else will protect either of those.

I am trying to find myself and my Soul in this Storm called Life. By the Grace of God, I will learn to Love Thyself first and be Happy once again!

November 16, 2020

~Twisted Madness~

Now that my Mind keeps going, going and won't Stop. It's Not the Good going either, it's the Twisted Bad going! It's the Side of Me that I Don't Like when She comes out to play! So you know you brought out a side of me that even I'm Afraid of! I sometimes Lose Focus and can't Control my Emotions. I have some Insanity going on right now that the Madness is Twisting all up in my Head with Hurtful and evil thoughts and trying to remain Calm all at the Same Time!

~Empty Vessel~

Why does it have to be like this? This shit sucks so bad! What did I do to deserve all this pain and anguish I feel deep down in my Soul? All these emotions and feelings are killing my Soul and Spirit! There is no more fight left in me at this moment to want to smile. There is no purposeful feeling left in my Soul to be whole and Sane, for Soul is slowly dying its making me shiver down to my Bones! Just when you thought your spirit may rise once again, there is that fear that comes true and your spirit gets stripped right out of you!

As your Soul and Spirit gets taken away so abruptly, your Heart and Mind goes into shock.

(Continued on Pg. 39)

Your Mind starts to spin so fast that you can't stop it and it's screaming out with Confusion!

Your Heart starts to beat painfully and slowly, feels like a knife went right through it while crying out with sadness! When the Heart and Mind gets hurt to the point when you can't stop crying, you know your Soul is in pain and only wants to find its way Home. While your Soul is slowly dying, you're killing the Spirit within yourself with so much Anguish. All I can do is cry!

I wonder what I did to deserve all this. I just want to find my Spirit to be able to go home to a Soul filled with Contentment and Stability! So, why when I deserve that but end up with feeling like I am never good enough for anything? These mixed feelings and emotions is burning my Body into an "Empty Vessel" that once was full of Life!

Shattered!

I can't even Fake a Smile anymore! My mom always said "Fake it till you make it!" She always put a smile on her face, faking as she's okay because she was strong on the outside. I try but on the inside, I am truly breaking! Deep down in my Heart, Mind, Soul and Spirit, everything is so disarrayed that I don't want to even put it all back together again. I just want to leave it all right where it is and go somewhere new!

December 1, 2020

Ecstatic with a Damaged Soul!

Why is it, that when things more positive is starting to happen for me and I can't express really how happy I am? Life in general is hard for me; I can't handle or pretend to be content anymore! I can't even put on a Fake Smile, just until I make it! I don't even know my Own Soul anymore!

My Mind is just one big maze and I am Lost! My Heart is just Beyond Confused! Internally I am genuinely ecstatic but my Soul is way too Damaged to show it externally!

Printed in the United States
By Bookmasters